CANCER
June 21–July 22

A
good head and
a good heart
are always a
formidable
combination

✦ Nelson Mandela ✦

IRIS

CANCER

Love is always available to me

summer

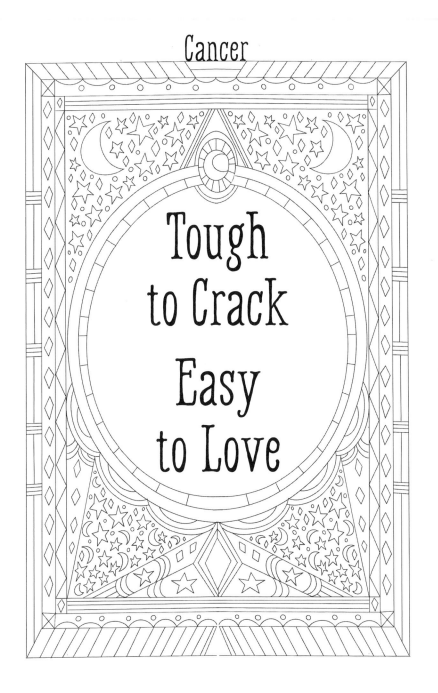

Tough
to Crack

Easy
to Love

Kind

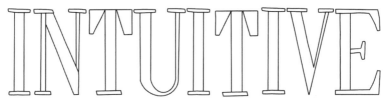

INTUITIVE

Protective

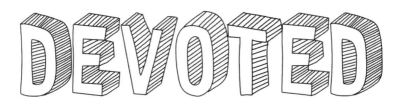

DEVOTED

PASSIONATE

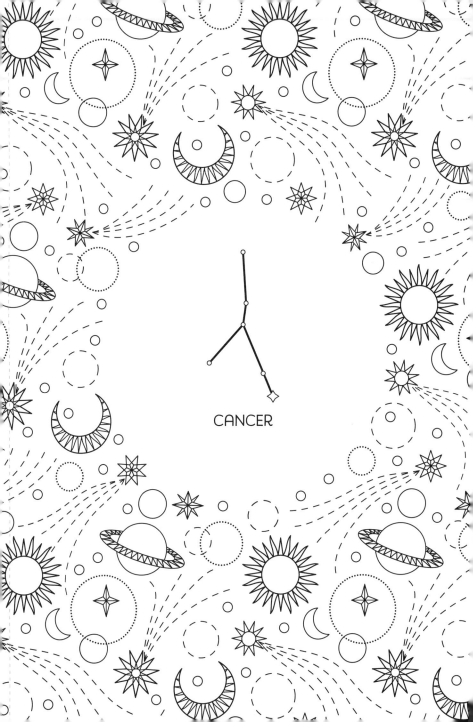

CANCER

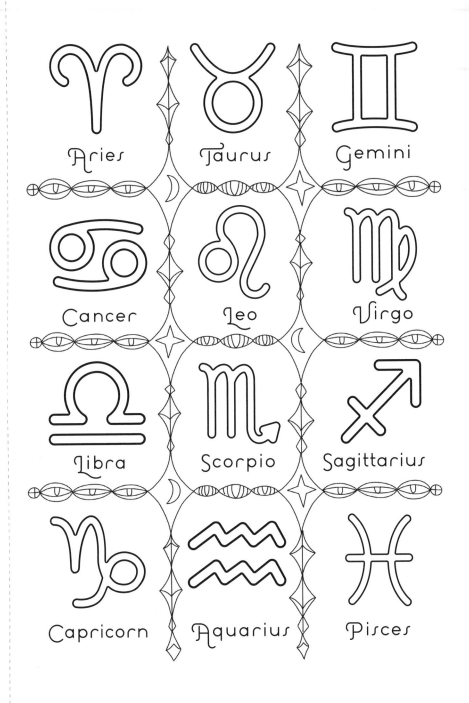

Aries

Taurus

Gemini

Cancer

Leo

Virgo

Libra

Scorpio

Sagittarius

Capricorn

Aquarius

Pisces

Water Signs

Cancer

Scorpio

Pisces

LET THE STARS LEAD THE WAY

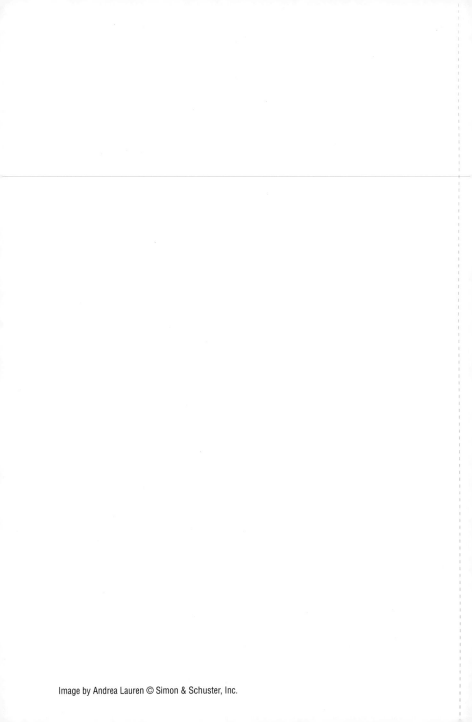